Published 1972 by
The Hamlyn Publishing Group Limited
London · New York · Sydney · Toronto
Hamlyn House, Feltham, Middlesex, England
© Copyright The Hamlyn Publishing Group Limited 1972

ISBN 0 600 36048 2

Photoset by BAS Printers Limited, Wallop, Hampshire, England
Printed by Litografia A. Romero, S.A.
Santa Cruz de Tenerife, Canary Islands (Spain)

**The illustrations in this book
have been selected from the
Hamlyn all-colour paperback
AIRCRAFT by John W. R. Taylor**

Spotlight on
Aircraft

by Graeme Cook
illustrated by Gerry Palmer

HAMLYN
LONDON · NEW YORK · SYDNEY · TORONTO

Above: One of the early winged gods

Below right: The legendary Daedalus and Icarus

Introduction

Ever since man could walk on his own two feet, he has tried to take yet another step – into the air! Watching the birds sweep through the air with grace and freedom, the envy man had for them heightened, and for thousands of years the ability to fly meant that a creature took a place amongst the gods and became something to be worshipped. Relics of those far-off days still remain, showing the gods which primitive man worshipped – having wings. These gods were pre-eminent over man for they could do the one thing that man could not – and that was to fly.

The craving to emulate the creatures that soared through the air became a fixation in men's minds, and so it was that, in their primitive way, they too tried to take to the air . . . always with disastrous results. Legends tell us many stories of men who, through the ages, have tried to lift themselves from the ground on wings.

Perhaps the best-known of all the early 'fliers' was Daedalus who, with his son Icarus, was imprisoned in a labyrinth by Minos, the King of Crete. There seemed to be no escape from their island prison until Daedalus had what he thought was a stroke of genius. He remembered the tales of ancient gods who were able to fly, so he decided that

he and his son would fly to freedom. He made two sets of wings with feathers, which he and his son attached to their arms with wax. But, however ingenious his idea might have been, Daedalus was to meet with problems.

Just before they took off from a tower, Daedalus warned his son that it would be dangerous to fly too close to the sun as the heat might melt his wax wings. But alas, Icarus became so enraptured with the thrill of flying that he soared too high into the sky and the sun melted his wax. The feathers peeled off his arms and he plunged to his death in the sea below, while his father flew on to safety in Italy.

Like so many legends, the flight of Daedalus and Icarus was pure fiction, but nevertheless the good people of the day, and many after them, were convinced that the story was true. Indeed, so firm was their belief in the possibility of flight that others tried to fly.

The most famous of the intrepid birdmen to make the attempt in Britain was Oliver of

Above: The monk of Malmesbury was among the first to attempt a flying leap from a tower

Below: A flapping wing machine, built by Jacob Degan, flew only because it had a balloon to lift it

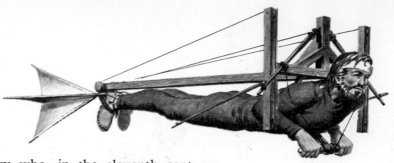

Malmesbury who, in the eleventh century, leapt from a tower, flapping his wings furiously, only to come to grief on the ground below, breaking almost every bone in his body. While in Scotland, the canny Scots were no less adventurous. John Damian thought he could 'fly like the birds' and found himself with more than a few broken bones. But Damian reasoned that he had failed because he had foolishly used chicken's feathers for his 'wings' and not those of high-flying birds. Chickens, he knew, were unable to fly more than a few feet into the air!

Many more were to make brave but fool-hardy attempts at flight, in spite of the failures of those who had gone before them, and it was not until the Italian, Leonardo da Vinci, set his mind to the problem that the first reasonably practical ideas were put forward. But although da Vinci was a genius and his ideas were the nearest thing that had

Above: Leonardo da Vinci's flying machine

Below: Early means of propulsion ranged from paddle wheels to geese, but none of the craft actually flew

been thought of to the flying machine, none of the aircraft that he designed flew, or would ever have flown, simply because in those days there were no engines capable of propelling such machines, and the materials he envisaged using were much too heavy for the job. In his thoughts on aviation da Vinci saw the power coming from the pilot, using his hands, arms and legs, but as we have seen, even in this century, human-powered flight over any great distance is impossible.

It took Jacob Degan to show the world how to fly and he claimed to have lifted himself off the ground by flapping a pair of improvised wings. What he did not tell his awe-struck admirers was that he had only succeeded in doing so with the aid of a giant balloon!

Above: Science fiction writer Cyrano de Bergerac wrote of space craft propelled by dew, and a man who could fly by fixing smoke bottles to his body

The first man credited with designing a flying aircraft was a Jesuit priest, Laurence de Gusamao. He built a glider which resembled a flying hen and, for the first time in recorded history, a model of his aeroplane actually flew at Lisbon in 1709. At last man had developed a design which actually flew. But he was a long way from bringing to perfection his means and manner of getting himself off the ground in his craft. The chapters that follow tell of the first successful flights, then trace the developments of various types of civilian aircraft up to the present day. The purpose of this volume is to tell the story of the peaceful uses of the aeroplane and not its function as a weapon of war, which in itself would occupy a complete book. So read on and enjoy the miracle of man's conquest of the air . . .

Balloons and Airships

The major breakthrough in manned flight came almost by accident when two brothers, Joseph and Etienne Montgolfier, sat gazing into their fire one evening in their home in France almost two hundred years ago. They remarked to each other how the small pieces of paper one of them had tossed on to the fire were lifted upwards by the smoke. They reasoned that if a tiny amount of smoke (or hot air) could lift paper into the air then surely a great deal of heat could do the same with larger pieces of material.

They lost no time in putting their theory to the test and took a small silk bag and held it with the open end over the fire. When they let the bag go, it immediately shot towards the roof. Perhaps, they thought, they had found the power which would lift man from the ground, and they began experimenting on a grander scale.

On the 5th of June, 1783, the brothers Montgolfier proved their theory by sending a balloon 38 ft. in diameter into the air, using the same principle they had employed with their silk bag. To the astonishment of the

Above: Joseph Montgolfier, one of the famous French brothers, with the balloon which carried a sheep, a cock and a duck on 19th September, 1783

Below: Blanchard and Jeffries became the first men to fly across the English Channel in their balloon on 7th January, 1785

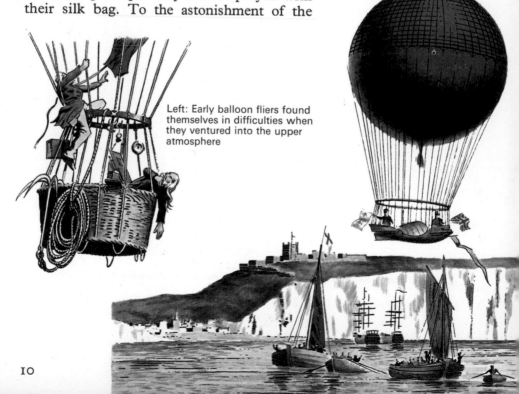

Left: Early balloon fliers found themselves in difficulties when they ventured into the upper atmosphere

Left: The first airship, powered by a 3-h.p. steam engine, was designed and flown by Henri Giffard in 1852. It had a top speed of 6 m.p.h. and made an epic flight from Paris to Trappes, but was found to lack the controllability which was vital to make it a success

onlookers, the balloon rose majestically higher and higher into the sky. From then on there was no holding them back and they embarked on even more adventurous projects. Their one ambition was to fly themselves, but like all sensible pioneers they wanted first to test their balloon properly before they personally took to the air. On the 19th of September in that same year, three living beings rose into the air suspended in a basket beneath a Montgolfier balloon; they were a duck, a cock and a sheep.

But it was a young doctor, Jean-Francois Pilatre de Rozier, who took his life in his hands and rose to a height of 85 ft. in the Montgolfier balloon to become the first man to actually fly. However, the enthusiastic men who flew in balloons that were to follow found that their craft had one serious drawback – it was at the mercy of the wind; once in the air, the wind could carry the balloon wherever it went. Man needed some form of power that he could command himself. It took another Frenchman, Henri Giffard, to come up with the answer. He built an enormous gas bag and suspended a gondola beneath it, and to this he

Below: Santos-Dumont, a Brazilian, was the first man to marry the petrol engine to the airship and in 1901 he won a 125,000-franc prize when he flew the airship shown here from Saint-Cloud, round the Eiffel Tower in Paris, and back in less than thirty minutes

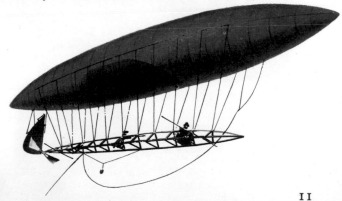

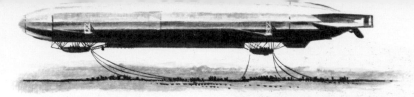

Above: Count Ferdinand von Zeppelin built and perfected the 'rigid' airship shown here. In 1910, he began the first ever regular air passenger service between Lake Constance and Berlin as well as other German cities. Before the outbreak of the First World War, Zeppelins had carried more than 35,000 passengers

Below: After the war, the Germans built the mighty *Graf Zeppelin* and the *Hindenburg*, both of which made trans-Atlantic flights to America. The luxurious and spacious accommodation on these airships has never since been matched. The *Hindenburg* burst into flames in America and 35 people died

attached a 3-h.p. steam engine and propeller. With this he was able to steer his craft, and so became the first man to fly what we call an airship.

The real turning-point in airship aviation came in 1898 when a Brazilian called Santos-Dumont married the airship to the petrol engine. His airship was what was known as non-rigid; that is, it relied upon the gas inside it to keep its shape. Then came the most lasting of all the true airships, the German Zeppelin, designed by Count Ferdinand von Zeppelin.

His construction differed from the Frenchman's in that it had a rigid framework inside which consisted of hollow compartments filled with gas. The entire construction was then covered with fabric. But although the Zeppelins got into service and were indeed the first real passenger-carrying aircraft plying between Europe and the Americas, they were to meet their doom when the mighty *Hindenburg*, the most spacious and luxurious of them all, caught fire at its mooring in America and thirty-five people lost their lives. From that moment on, the airship was no longer regarded as a really safe means of travel.

Right: The first powered aircraft to hop with a pilot at the controls was built by a French naval officer, Felix du Temple, and flown by one of his young sailors

Above: The wind tunnel in which the Wright Brothers tested various wing sections until they found the best one for their aircraft

Above: The Wright Brothers' engine, which they designed specially for the *Flyer*

Below: Orville Wright's epic first flight which took place on 17th December, 1903

First Flights

In spite of the successes with the airship, and while man strove to perfect it, others aimed their talents in a different direction, concentrating on the heavier-than-air aeroplane. Many attempts were made at building such a craft and most of them met with disastrous results; but in 1857 a French Naval officer, Felix du Temple, designed and built a model aeroplane with a propeller at the front which was powered by a steam engine . . . and it actually flew. At least, he realised, he had struck on the right design for heavier-than-air flight. Seventeen years later he built a full-sized version which flew for a short hop but only after it had gathered speed by racing down a slope.

Several 'hoppers' followed but the day that everyone had awaited so long did not come until 1903 when two American brothers who had been experimenting with gliders fitted an engine to their biplane *Flyer* glider. At 10.35 a.m. on the 17th of December, 1903, Orville Wright piloted the aeroplane into the air and

became the first man ever to fly a heavier-than-air plane off level ground under its own power. The flight lasted 12 seconds, during which time the aircraft flew 120 ft. Not much of a flight by present day standards, but a major step forward in man's bid to conquer the air.

The Wrights' aircraft made four flights that day, the last of which covered 852 ft., and the brothers' success showed without question that man could and would master the air. Three years later, in Europe, Santos-Dumont led the way for the European pioneers when he flew his *14 bis*, a comical-looking aircraft which flew tail first. Other and better flying machines quickly followed, like Henri Farman's Voisin biplane which made the first circular flight of more than a kilometre; in 1908 Glenn Curtiss, an American designer, flew his *June Bug* more than a mile and won a trophy for doing so.

Above: Santos-Dumont became the first man in Europe to fly a powered aeroplane when he took to the air in this cumbersome craft on 23rd October, 1906. His aircraft not only looked ungainly because of its box construction but actually flew *tail first*!

Till that year no British aircraft designer had met with any success, but A. V. Roe, one of the fathers of British aviation, built and flew his triplane to become the first Briton to fly an all-British aeroplane in England.

By then fliers were becoming even more ambitious and the first-ever air race was held at Rheims, in France, where a collection of varying types took part before a quarter of a million spectators. But the crowning achievement of that year took place on the 25th of July when Louis Blériot took off from Calais, on the French coast, and flew across the English Channel in his Blériot XI monoplane – the first man and plane ever to do so.

The age of the aerial trail-blazers was close at hand.

Above: One of the most famous of all the early flights was that of Blériot's across the English Channel on 25th July, 1909, in his XI monoplane when he flew from Baraques, near Calais, to a meadow alongside Dover Castle

Below: The first-ever air race was held at Rheims, in France, in 1909. Leading here is an Antoinette, followed by a Wright biplane, a Curtiss Golden Flyer, a Voisin, a Blériot XI and another Voisin

The Pathfinders

The first of the successful flying trail-blazers were Captain John Alcock and Lieutenant Arthur Whitten-Brown who, in June 1919, flew non-stop across the Atlantic Ocean.

They left Newfoundland at 4.15 p.m. on the 14th of June in a converted twin-engined Vickers Vimy bomber and almost immediately flew into terrible weather conditions. Their aircraft was lashed by driving rain and tossed about the sky by tempestuous gales. Then to make matters even worse, the radio broke down and they were completely alone and unable to call for help if disaster should befall them.

As they droned on over the wild sea, ice began forming on the wings, causing the aircraft to dive, out of control, towards the waves. The Vimy actually hit the waves several times before Alcock miraculously succeeded in getting control once more.

After 16½ hours' flying through these terrible conditions, they sighted land and crash-landed in a bog in Ireland.

Inspired by the success of Alcock and

Above: The converted Vickers Vimy bomber in which Alcock and Brown made the first non-stop crossing of the Atlantic by air in June 1919 and blazed a trail for the airliners that were to follow

Above: Kingsford Smith's Fokker monoplane, first across the Pacific Ocean in 1928

Left: The most famous flight of all time was carried out by Charles Lindbergh in May 1927 when he made the first solo crossing of the Atlantic in his Ryan monoplane *Spirit of St Louis*

Brown, other aviators took to the air. Two Australians, Ross and Smith, flew from Hounslow, in England, to Port Darwin, Australia, in 28 days, flying in a series of hops. Then in 1926, Lieutenant Commander Richard Byrd of the United States Navy scored a first when he flew over the North Pole.

But the most celebrated achievement of all came in May 1927 when Charles Lindbergh, flying a Ryan monoplane, named *Spirit of St. Louis*, flew the Atlantic from America to France – alone.

The following year, Charles Kingsford Smith and Charles Ulm flew the 6850 miles from San Francisco across the Pacific Ocean to Brisbane, Australia, in their Fokker Monoplane, *Southern Cross*.

The intrepid Commander Byrd achieved a double in 1928 when he made the second of his epic flights, this time across the South Pole.

It was the fearless men like these who braved the unknown and led the way for the great jets of today.

Above: Lt. Cdr. Richard Byrd, having become the first man to fly across the North Pole in 1926, created a double when he flew across the South Pole in this Ford Tri-motor in 1929

Left: The Houston-Westland PV-3 was the first aeroplane to fly over the world's highest mountain, Mount Everest. It did so on 3rd April, 1933, at a height of 34,000 ft.

The First Airliners

As early as 1911, cargo and mail were being carried in aircraft, but it was not until after the end of the First World War that men seriously considered carrying passengers in aeroplanes. The first to enter the airline business were the Germans, who opened a daily service between Berlin and Weimer using converted bombers. But it had its drawbacks. The two passengers it carried sat in open cockpits!

The French soon followed suit when the famous Farman Company opened a regular service between Paris and Brussels, using the giant Goliath aircraft which had an enclosed cabin as well as a considerable degree of comfort. The comfort of the passenger was beginning to be given the importance it deserved but the first real international air service was not exactly luxurious. A British airline, Aircraft Transport and Travel Limited, flew four passengers at a time from

Above: One of the earliest airliners, a DH9 of Air Transport and Travel Ltd., had open cockpits for the passengers who had to be well wrapped up against the bitter cold of the wind

Below: The French Farman Goliath helped pioneer the idea of passenger comfort with its enclosed cabins. The aircraft shown here was operated by Air Union, a predecessor of Air France

aeroplanes. But these were a far cry from
modern airliners and, like the German aircraft, they had open cockpits in which the
passengers sat huddled and muffled against
the icy blast of the wind. Some even took along
hot-water bottles on the 2½ hour flight.

However, the airline services gradually improved, albeit rather slowly, when more
comfortable aircraft were introduced along
with other innovations like radio, which not
only helped pilots in the event of an emergency
but also allowed them to check their position
while they were flying.

Aerodromes bore little or no resemblance

Below, top: A German single-
engined AEG J.11 of the type
used by the Deutsche Luft-
Reederie on its daily passenger
service between Berlin and
Weimar in 1919

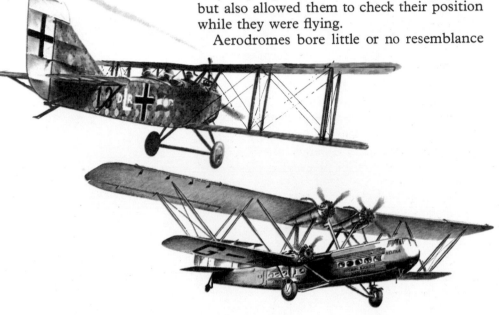

to the sprawling airports of today. A cluster
of huts on a field was all that marked most of
the airports. Air Traffic Control was almost
non-existent with aircraft colliding in mid-air
because there was no alert system to warn
pilots of approaching planes.

The real turning point came when the
private airlines were finally helped financially
by the government. This meant that at last
they could afford the improvements they so
desperately needed.

Until then there was no reliable way of
accurately forecasting the weather and many
pilots had to judge for themselves whether or

Above: This early four-engined
giant Handley Page H.P.42 went
into service with Britain's
Imperial Airways in 1931. Seven
more were built, some of which
operated on the Britain-India
route as well as between London
and Paris

Right: The first aeroplane to carry a cargo was this Valkyrie B, piloted by Horatio Barber. Its cargo is reputed to have consisted of a box of Osram lamps which Barber transported from Shoreham to Hove, Sussex, on 4th July, 1911

not the weather would hold on a long run. One strange tale is told of how KLM pilots who were about to fly over the sea had to first fly low over a cottage on the coast where a message on a blackboard would tell them if the weather over the sea was suitable to fly in!

As more money became available so the flights became safer, and with the introduction of the four-engined passenger aircraft, safety in the air improved dramatically, along with passenger comfort.

The huge Handley Page HP 42 biplane was a fine example of the new luxury airliner, with its comfortable cabins in which meals were served by stewards. Commercial air transport had come to stay and many more people were taking advantage of travel by air as more and more routes were opened up.

Below: In aircraft like this D.H.4, pilots employed by the United States Mail Service fought their way through almost unbelievably bad weather to deliver mail. Of the first forty pilots recruited for this job, thirty of them were killed

Seaplanes and Flying Boats

In the early days of flying there were no true runways, as we know them today, and the pioneer flights were generally made from grass fields. As most of these fields were on farmland and vital to the country's economy, aircraft designers looked to the vast expanses of sea as a possible landing and take-off place for their aircraft.

So it was that the idea of the seaplane was born.

The first man to successfully fly a seaplane was Henri Fabre, who attached three floats to his aeroplane. His pioneering flight took place in 1910 but it was regarded as something of a fluke because he was unable to repeat his initial success. However, he had set other designers thinking and the American Glenn Curtiss flew the first really practical seaplane in 1911.

Three years later a passenger air service

Above: Henri Fabre pioneered the idea of the float plane which could take off and land on water. He made the first flight off water in this strange aircraft in 1910

Below, top: A Short C Class flying-boat of Imperial Airways which entered service with the company in 1936

Below, bottom: One of the big Sikorsky amphibious flying boats operated by Pan American on its early Atlantic and Pacific routes

began on a lake in the United States, using a two-seat flying-boat which transported passengers from one side of the lake to the other. This aircraft differed from the seaplane in that the underpart of the fuselage was shaped like a ship's hull and it was this which sat in the water while two stabilising floats were attached at the tip of each of the lower wings of the biplane.

The flying-boat developed quite rapidly and in 1919 a Curtiss (named after the American pilot) in service with the United States Navy made the first crossing of the Atlantic by flying in stages via the Azores.

The idea of flying-boats caught on with most of the big countries of the world and, during the 1930s, they were used extensively for trans-ocean flying.

The flying-boat had its hey-day in those years and some truly luxurious aircraft were built which gave passengers comfortable flights to many countries in the world. Britain's Imperial Airways built up a fleet of twenty-eight of the new Short C Class Empire flying-

Above: This monster is the Italian Caproni Ca 60 which had a wing-span of 100 ft. and made only two very brief flights over Lake Maggiore in March 1921

Below: One of the most remarkable and yet successful ideas during the flying-boat era was this one where a seaplane rode piggy-back on a flying-boat until after take-off. Then the two separated and the seaplane flew to its destination

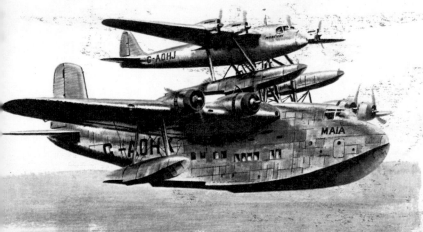

Above: The seaplane *Mercury* is seen here parting company with flying-boat *Maia* after being lifted into the air. Because of this unusual method of take-off, the *Mercury* was able to carry more fuel and broke a long-distance flying record

boats powered by four engines, while in America the Boeing 314A was opening new and regular routes across the Pacific Ocean.

But the real 'jumbo' of the flying-boat era was the German Dornier DOX which was the largest aircraft of its time, powered by no less than *twelve* engines and capable of carrying 150 passengers. But alas, like many of these giants, it met with limited success, achieving little more than an almost disastrous trans-Atlantic flight.

Perhaps the most novel flying-boat experiment came in 1938. Designers knew that aircraft can fly at a greater weight than that at which they can take off from the ground, and a bright designer thought up the idea of a fuel-laden seaplane riding piggy-back on a flying-boat for take off, then separating when airborne, thus giving it a longer range because of its increased fuel load. The idea may

Below: The biggest aeroplane of its time was the German Dornier Do X flying-boat which was powered by twelve engines and was capable of carrying 150 passengers on a trans-Atlantic flight. It first saw service in 1929

Above: A Short Solent 4 flying-boat of Tasman Empire Airways. Until 1958, the Solent was one of the most popular of all the flying-boats but now only a few remain in airline service, mainly in New Zealand

Below: One of the smaller passenger-carrying seaplanes is the Grumman Widgeon. The one shown here operates in New Zealand, taking tourists on sight-seeing trips

sound crazy but it actually worked and in 1938 the seaplane *Mercury*, sitting atop the flying boat *Maia*, took off from Dundee, Scotland, then separated and flew the 5998 miles to South Africa, setting up a long-distance record which has never been beaten.

Although today the big jets have taken over the routes once flown by flying-boats, there are still some in service in countries like Canada and New Zealand, where they ply between the great lakes.

Above: Otto Lilienthal, the German glider designer, made thousands of successful flights during the 19th century in the two gliders seen here

Above: Octave Chanute, the designer and pilot of this biplane glider, did much to inspire the Wright Brothers in their flying

Right: Percy Pilcher, an Englishman and an exponent of the 'hang' glider, built the graceful Hawk and first flew it in 1896

Gliders

Today many thousands of men and women enjoy the thrill of soaring through the air in graceful gliders, experiencing a sport which is ever-increasing in popularity as more and more young people qualify as glider pilots.

The origin of the glider dates back many hundreds of years to the time when the Chinese invented and flew kites. These ancient kites flew on much the same principle as the gliders of today, making use of the wind and up-currents of air to keep them airborne. But it was an Englishman, Sir George Cayley, who, towards the end of the eighteenth century, built and flew the first model glider which consisted of a long pole with a wing mounted above it and a movable cruciform tail. In 1853, he built a full-sized version with some modifications in design and his coachman flew the craft across a valley on Caley's estate ... then promptly resigned, terrified at his experience!

It was a German, Otto Lilienthal, who, inspired by Cayley's success, designed and built his own gliders in which he made thousands of flights.

Lilienthal's gliders varied in design; one was a biplane and the other a monoplane. He piloted them by hanging beneath them and controlling them by swinging his body to and fro, and in that way manoeuvring them about

the sky. But alas, the fate that befell many of these pioneering pilots also came to Lilienthal when, in 1896, he fell from one of his gliders as it soared through the air and crashed to his death.

In England and America, Lilienthal had his followers who devoutly continued his work even after his untimely death. Most notable among these were Percy Pilcher, an Englishman, and the American Octave Chanute, both of whom built and flew gliders designed on the principle laid down by Lilienthal and each of them made their mark in aviation history.

It was largely because of what they read of the efforts and success of these intrepid glider pilots that Wilbur and Orville Wright became fascinated by the thoughts of manned

Above: Gliding is fast growing in popularity and the scene shown here is typical of many spots all over the country where gliding clubs have been established

Below: Up until the Second World War, Germany led the field in glider design and this one, a Vampyr of 1921, was one of their successes

flight and in the beginning they, too, set about building and flying gliders. Their eventual success in becoming the first men to fly a heavier-than-air powered aircraft was a direct result of their experiments with gliders and it was to one of their gliders that they fitted their engine which took them on that epoch-making flight in 1903.

But the coming of the powered aircraft by no means halted the advance of the glider and its design. Indeed, the interest and enthusiasm for gliders rose to its first peak in the 1920s when young Germans took an interest in gliding.

Below: The Minimoa, one of the most graceful of all the German gliders

Throughout the 1920s and the early 1930s

the popularity of the glider grew in Germany and pilots became more skilled in manoeuvring their craft about the sky. As their knowledge of aerodynamics increased, so the design of gliders improved and soon they were flying aircraft not unlike the gliders we can see in Britain today.

There are many different types of gliders in use by clubs today, ranging from the rather spartan trainers, in which pupil pilots train, to the sleek and elegant highly sophisticated record breakers which compete in the annual World Glider Championships.

Above: Even before the war the Germans were producing gliders, like this Olympia, which would have done credit to modern designs

27

Light Aircraft

Single- and twin-engined light aircraft play an ever-increasing part in today's world of aviation not only for the business executive who has to dash from one part of the country to the other on urgent business, but for the amateur pilot who spends his weekends taking to the air just for the thrill of flying.

The most famous of all these small aeroplanes is the Tiger Moth, a single-engined biplane which for over twenty years provided the RAF with its initial trainer for pupil pilots. Many of the men who fly today's Jumbo jets and airliners look back with affection to their training on the old Tiger, so much so, in fact, that there is a 'Tiger Club' for devotees of the Tiger Moth.

Above: The most famous of all the light planes is the Tiger Moth, which as well as serving as a trainer with the RAF for many years proved ideal for stunt flying at air shows

Below: Three of the popular light aircraft carrying out a wide variety of flying duties are Britain's Beagle Pup (above); the Short Skyvan (below left); and the Cessna Skymaster (below right) with its push-and-pull propellers

Such was the versatility and manoeuvrability of the Tiger that, on the 25th anniversary of Blériot's epic flight across the English Channel, a young pilot called Geoffrey Tyson flew across the Channel *upside down* in a Tiger.

The Tiger Moth led to the development of better and more efficient light aircraft which came to be used for business and pleasure, and most of the major countries of the world concentrated their efforts on the development of the light aircraft, but none more than the United States where it is estimated that more than twelve thousand of these little planes are built every year.

Above: These two aircraft are each capable of carrying ten passengers on short-haul journeys. They are the Italian Piaggio P166B Portofino, at the top of the picture, and the Britten-Norman Islander

Below: More than half of the world's light aircraft are built by the Cessna company of the United States, and the two seen here are amongst the most popular of their designs: the single-engined Skylane and the bigger twin-engined Skynight

Helicopters

Above: The fore-runners of today's helicopters were these strange craft. They were Paul Cornu's tandem rotor machine and the Breguet-Richet Gyroplane, both of which were flown in France in 1907

Below: One of the original helicopters built in 1910 by the man who was to become the greatest helicopter designer in the world — Igor Sikorsky

It was Leonardo da Vinci, the greatest genius of all time, who first thought of the idea of the helicopter. Although his design for an aircraft that would rise straight into the air was totally impracticable and could not possibly have worked, even if he had had a proper power unit for it, the germ of an idea was there and it was because he put it down on paper that many years later the possibility of a practical helicopter was considered.

After the turn of the last century, when fixed-wing aeroplanes were coming into their own and better and more efficient models were being designed, the problem of runways was being considered. While aeroplanes were able to cover greater distances, their extending range meant that they had to carry more fuel and this meant that they were heavier. The result was that they needed longer runways on which to take off. This set the designers thinking and they pondered on the idea of an aircraft that could take off vertically into the air, thus doing away with the neccessity for a runway. The helicopter was the obvious answer. The principle of vertical take-off was first appreciated by two Frenchmen who designed the Breguet-Richet Gyroplane No. 1 and flew it in 1907, but it had been held steady by four men. Yet another Frenchman had greater success. He was Paul Cornu, who built a tandem rotor machine but was unable

Above: Juan de la Cierva built this autogyro in 1927. It differed from the helicopter in that it had a conventional engine and propeller, but the free-rotating blades above it gave it a short take-off distance

Above: Leonardo da Vinci's original design for a helicopter

Below: Sikorsky's VS-300 seen here hovering during trials in 1940

to continue his experiments because of the lack of money.

The great breakthrough in vertical take-off aircraft came when Juan ′ de la Cierva, a Spaniard, invented and flew his Autogiro. This aeroplane vaguely resembled a conventional monoplane, but mounted on top of it was a rotor blade which was turned automatically by the forces of the wind. Although this aeroplane could not take off vertically, it could rise into the air in a much shorter distance than the conventional aircraft.

But Cierva's Autogiro was not without its problems. His first design tended to slur sideways and it was not until he perfected the flapping rotor, in which each of the four blades of the rotor was hinged at the root, did he overcome the difficulty.

In the 1930s German designers led the field in helicopter development, but the man who can really claim the title of 'father of the helicopter' did not seriously begin experimenting until 1939. He was Igor Sikorsky

Above: A Sikorsky CH 54A Skycrane delivering its Universal Military pod

Above: A Westland Wessex flying crane takes a heavy gun into action while, below, a Sikorsky UH 34 retrieves an astronaut from the sea

who, in 1910, had built an experimental machine but had then switched his attentions to fixed-wing aircraft. When he finally returned to helicopter design he produced the VS-300, which was built of steel tubing and powered by a 75-h.p. Lycoming engine. It consisted of a three-blade main rotor with an anti-torque rotor on the tail. This secondary rotor prevented the aircraft from swinging round in circles on its own axis because of the power of the main rotor, a problem earlier helicopter designers had faced and failed to solve.

To Sikorsky, the VS-300 was merely a test-bed and he produced an improved version, the R-4, not long after. It was this aircraft which was to prove the foundation for the world's helicopter industry and pave the way for the helicopters of today.

More than any other type of aircraft, the helicopter is capable of fulfilling a great many different and varying tasks, both in the military and civilian fields of aviation. Since Sikorsky perfected the principle of the helicopter it has grown to be the perfect workhorse of the sky, carrying out such tasks as air-sea rescue, crop-spraying, car and passenger transportation, as well as picking up astronauts from the sea, to mention just a few.

Both America and Russia over the past few years have led the field in helicopter development, producing machines capable of lifting enormous weights. Typical of these is the Sikorsky CH-54, which can lift a load of ten tons or more, and the Russian Mil Mi-10, which proved its strength when it lifted a

Right: British European Airways use this Sikorsky S-69N to ferry passengers to and from the Scilly Isles

Above: A Westland Whirlwind rescues a ditched pilot from his rubber dinghy while the huge Russian Mil Mi-10 (below) proves its strength by lifting a coach on a platform strung beneath it

motor coach on a platform suspended beneath it. An even bigger version of the same aircraft set up a world record when it lifted a forty-ton payload.

As a military aircraft the 'chopper', as the helicopter is commonly called, has been adapted as both a gun-ship and a commando carrier. Fitted with a variety of armaments ranging from machine-guns to rockets and bombs, it is capable of delivering surprise attacks on enemy units in jungle, while the heavier type, notably the Westland Wessex, can carry commando strike forces into the heart of enemy territory.

But perhaps the most promising future for the helicopter lies in the field of passenger transportation from airport to city centre. On many occasions the benefit of fast air travel is lost when passengers have to travel by car or train from an airport to their destination in the city and the helicopter is fast overcoming this problem by running short-haul flights to and from the busy airports which almost always lie miles outside the big cities of the world.

Aeroplanes at Work

Above: This Stearman Model 75 is seen here spraying crops with insecticide to kill pests, a job that demands great flying skill from the pilot

The light single- and twin-engined aeroplanes which have grown in popularity so dramatically in recent years are not merely the playthings of amateur pilots, nor are they restricted in use to the business executive. They have been adapted to perform many tasks and have proved invaluable in a wide variety of roles.

Perhaps the most famous of all these roles is that of the air ambulance in the Australian outback. This vital service was begun by a minister, John Flynn, who, in 1927, recognised the need for a medical service for the farmers who lived and worked in the remote and desolate regions of Australia. He hired a DH 50 aircraft, along with a crew, from the QANTAS airline, and operated a shuttle-service to ferry patients to hospital from these lonely out-posts. So was born the Royal Flying Doctor Service which still operates effectively today.

Below: A de Havilland Drover of the Royal Flying Doctor Service in the Australian outback. Inset: a doctor gives a patient urgent medical attention while the aircraft races to hospital

Light aircraft are also used in the war on insect pests. Fitted with special tanks, these aircraft sweep low over crops and spray them

Above: Another of the many jobs given to light aircraft is searching for minerals in inaccessible country. This specially adapted Piper Aztec carries survey equipment which enables scientists to detect mineral deposits

with insecticide, killing the tiny insects which can do so much damage to crops. The men who fly these aircraft are amongst the most skilled of all pilots because they have to fly so close to the ground that there is almost no safety margin should they get into difficulties.

Light aircraft mount non-stop patrols over the vast expanses of the Canadian forests, keeping watch on them lest fire should break out. In the event of such an alert, special twin-engined Canadair CL-215 aircraft are called in to 'bomb' the fires with water to prevent them spreading. Some of these aircraft also carry parachutists – called Smokejumpers – who drop into the forest and tackle the fire on the ground.

The versatility of the light aircraft is almost limitless and civilisation owes a great deal to these aeroplanes and the men who fly them.

Below: This Canadair CL-215 carries an unusual cargo of water bombs, which it rains down on forest fires when they break out in the vast wooded expanses of Canada. Aircraft like this have saved Canada from disaster on many occasions

The Coming of the Airliner

It was in the United States that the idea of the modern airliner as we know it today was born, perhaps surprisingly, during the hey-day of the flying-boat in the 1930s. The aircraft manufacturers realised that the flying-boat was of little use to airlines for inter-city domestic flights since not all the major cities had stretches of water suitable as landing places for these aircraft. It was obvious therefore that they had to concentrate on building landplane airliners capable of flying the short haul and coast-to-coast routes.

In Germany in the early 1930s the Junkers Ju52, a triple-engined monoplane, came into service with the Lufthansa airline and proved

Above: The Douglas DC-3, known in Britain as the Dakota, is the most successful airliner ever built and remained in service almost continuously for thirty years

Below: The Junkers Ju 52 went into service in Germany as a civilian transport aircraft in the early 1930s and later was converted into a wartime bomber

Above: One of the first of the 'luxury' airliners was the Armstrong Whitworth Argosy which, during the 1920s, saw service with Imperial Airways on the Middle East routes and often landed at desert runways

such a success that designers in America went for single-wing aeroplanes rather than the biplanes which had been built before. Furthermore the greatest revolution in aircraft construction was taking place at that time. No longer were the airliners built of wood. The age of the all-metal aeroplane had begun and with it came the most famous airliner ever to be designed and built – the Douglas DC-3, known in Britain as the Dakota.

The story of the Dakota has become almost a legend since it first came into service in 1936. No other aircraft has remained in service as long as the DC-3; indeed there are still some in operation even today.

The transformation from wooden-built to metal aircraft was the major turning point in aircraft construction. Aeroplanes were more reliable and remained longer in service, a fact

Below: Typical of the early airports was this one at Croydon, in England, showing a de Havilland Albatross parked near the control tower

Above: The transformation from wooden-frame aircraft to metal-built brought with it new problems for aircraft designers, seen inset, at their drawing board. It also meant that the builders had to acquire new skills in manufacturing the huge wing sections

Below: The gleaming shell of an all-metal airliner under construction at the aircraft factory

that is borne out only too clearly by the history of the DC-3, one of the first of the all-metal aircraft.

Techniques in aircraft building were fast becoming more exacting with the introduction of metal aircraft. No more 'hammer-and-nail stuff' but precise and accurate construction was vital.

In 1940, just after the beginning of the

Second World War, came another development which was to have a tremendous impact
on air passenger travel – the introduction of
the pressurised cabin. This meant that the
aircraft was 'sealed' and the pressure in the
cabin kept constant, allowing the pilot to fly
at greater altitudes above the bumpy and
turbulent air near the ground. The result was
a more comfortable flight for the passengers.

The first airliner to enter service with a
pressurised cabin was the Boeing 307 Strato-
liner which operated on the American domestic
routes.

Although the big piston-engined airliners
were all now metal built, the builders of the
smaller, short haul passenger aircraft tended
to stick to wood and fabric as the basics for

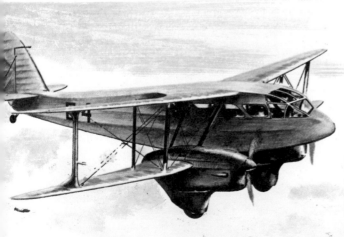

Left: For many years the de
Havilland DH Dragon Rapide
was a favourite short-haul
airliner and even now can still
be seen at flying clubs throughout the country in private
ownership

Above: The Bristol Brabazon 1, built at a cost of £3 million, was a flop and eventually was scrapped without ever getting into service

their aeroplanes. The most famous of these was the British DH 89 Dragon Rapide, an eight-seater biplane and one which is still used throughout the world, mostly by flying clubs and private owners.

The Second World War saw perhaps the greatest leap forward in aviation with the invention of radar, the all-seeing electronic eye which could penetrate darkness or bad

weather and 'point the way' for aircraft. On the ground in control towers at airports it enabled controllers to track aircraft and guide them in for safe landings. With this new innovation, airliners could be 'talked down' to smooth landings in bad visibility, where before they would have had to divert to another airfield where the visibility was clear.

There were no civilian airlines in Britain during the war and it was not until 1945, when the war in Europe was over, that the aircraft designers could once more turn their skills to producing airliners. A great deal of knowledge had been gained from the building of heavy bombers during the war years and the first

Above: The Vickers Viking was adapted from the wartime Wellington bomber and proved to be one of the most successful British airliners ever built

Below: The Boeing Stratocruiser was a two-deck adaptation of the B-29 bomber which dropped the atomic bombs on Japan at the end of the Second World War

passenger aircraft constructed in Britain after the war was based to a very large extent on the Wellington bomber. This was the Vickers Viking, an aircraft which, during the ten years that followed, was to pay its way handsomely for its operators, British European Airways.

Another of the highly successful aircraft developed from a wartime bomber was the four-engined Boeing Stratocruiser, a two-deck version of the Boeing B-29 bomber.

Not all the post-war designs were successes. A veritable giant of an aircraft, the 130-ton Bristol Brabazon was built at a cost of £3 million, but although it flew it never saw service and ended up in the breakers' yard.

Throughout the 1950s the United States continued to lead the world in big airliner design, producing the famous Douglas aircraft and the Lockheed Constellations, like the DC-7 and the Lockheed Super Constellation. But their days were numbered, for the age of the jet airliner was drawing near.

Above: These three aircraft came from the famous American Douglas family and were four-engined developments of the DC-3 Dakota. They are, reading from top to bottom, the DC-4, DC-6, and DC-7. All three of them operated on trans-Atlantic routes

Below: Another of the great American piston-engined airliners was the Super Constellation, which saw service with BOAC on its London—New York routes

Freighters

The fast transportation of freight by air grew in popularity after the war and to cope with the demand for this type of service, companies bought up wartime transports and converted them into freighters. Typical of this kind of aircraft were the Avro York and the DC-3 Dakota. But as useful as these aeroplanes undoubtedly were, they could act only as a stop-gap. It was obvious that new aircraft would have to be designed and built specially for the job of carrying cargo.

The concept of specially-built cargo planes

Above, left: The Avro York transport aircraft, seen taking off, was a development of the wartime Lancaster bomber. On the far right sits the most famous of all the transports, the adapted DC-3, with its side cargo doors open

Below: The Fairchild Packet pioneered modern quick-loading techniques with its hinged rear-loading doors

was not a new one and, as early as the 1920s, designs had been put forward for an aircraft with a hinged rear fuselage which would swing to one side to allow easy and quick loading. But it was not until many years later that the idea was finally put to use.

In order to take big and bulky loads it was important that the maximum height and width of the aircraft's interior should be open to access and, in pioneering this idea, the Fairchild company built their C-82 Packet which was basically a big 'pod' on wings between two tail booms. Both sides of the back of the pod were hinged and could be drawn open to allow cargo to be lifted in or motor vehicles to drive straight in.

The British Bristol Freighter was the first of the open-nose type of freighter. Its huge nose opened up like a gaping mouth to eat-up its cargo. So successful was this aircraft, that a bigger superfreighter was built which could carry a greater payload.

One of the most profitable uses to which

Below: The Bristol 170 Freighter, with its cargo doors in the nose, could carry both freight and passengers and operated on the highly-successful cross-channel route, ferrying cars between England and France

the Bristol Freighter was put was ferrying cars across the English Channel, speeding motor-tourists quickly on their way to tours of the Continent, saving them valuable time.

The greatest example of the use of air freighting came in 1948 when the beleaguered city of Berlin was kept alive by aircraft flying in food and essential supplies. During the year that the siege lasted, almost 2½ million tons of supplies were flown into the city – a tremendous achievement and one that proved once and for all the enormous potential of the air freighter.

Below: The versatility of the modern Lockheed Hercules now in service with the RAF is illustrated by its ability to carry heavy payloads and drop supplies quickly and accurately to ground troops

A refinement of some of the earlier freight-liner designs came when the Lockheed Hercules transport was built. In this aircraft, the rear of the cabin was made in the form of an upswept door which was hinged at the forward edge so that it swung downwards and served the dual purpose of a back door and a loading ramp. In the military version of this aircraft, many of which are in service with the RAF, the rear door can be opened in flight so that vehicles and supplies can be pushed out to float to the ground by parachute to troops on the ground.

Above: Another of the big transporters in service with the RAF is the Short Belfast, which can carry a payload of 35 tons at speeds up to 350 m.p.h.

Below: Canadair's swing-tail CL-44D4 freighter opens at the rear to allow easy access for cargo loading

The Lockheed C-5A Galaxy is the biggest and heaviest aircraft in the world (see page 49) and although it is a military aircraft it is nevertheless a transporter and capable of carrying payloads in excess of 100 tons. Unlike any other aircraft, the Galaxy's nose lifts upwards rather like the visor on a knight's helmet.

The most unusual looking freighter to take to the air must be the Super Guppy which was designed to perform a task no other freight-liner could do: to transport sections of the mighty American moon rockets from their place of manufacture to their launch sites. It could be said that the Guppy takes the rockets on the first stage of their journey to the moon!

The business of freight-carrying by air grows steadily bigger and already designers are planning aeroplanes, even greater than the mighty Galaxy, which will be capable of carrying vast payloads over longer distances.

Above: Surely the strangest aircraft flying today, the Super Guppy was built specially to carry American moon rockets from the factory to the launch site

Below: The DC-7F is a converted DC-7 airliner which has two doors at either end of the fuselage into which cargo can be loaded

The Jet Age

It is staggering to realise that the concept of the first really practical jet engine was born in 1928, when a young RAF officer cadet wrote a paper on 'Future Developments in Aircraft Design'. He was Frank Whittle, a man with incredible foresight, who saw a time when aeroplanes would be able to fly at almost 500 m.p.h. in the rarified atmosphere high above sea-level.

Whittle worked day and night designing an engine, but it was not until 1941 that it was tested in an aircraft, the specially-designed Gloster E28/39. The success of Whittle's engine was dramatic and the first British twin-engined fighter, the Meteor, was eventually brought into service. But the war was ended before the Meteor could play any really big part in it. The jet, however, was here to stay and, in 1952, a fully jet-powered de Havilland Comet of BOAC went into

Above: The Gloster E28/39 was the aircraft in which Frank Whittle's jet engine (inset) was tested. Experiments led to the introduction of the jet into the modern airliner and brought with it the fast, comfortable air travel we enjoy today

Below: A Lufthansa Vickers Viscount which was powered by turbo-prop engines, variations of the pure jet engine

service on the London-Johannesburg route, the first jet in the world to do so.

There was, however, another kind of 'jet' making a name for itself. This was the turbo-prop engine; unlike the pure jet which was designed to produce jet-thrust, the gas turbine in the turboprop engine was used to turn a conventional propeller. Aircraft using these engines did not have the speed of those using

Above: Russia's Tupolev Tu 104, one of the early jet airliners

Below: The de Havilland Comet, the first ever jet airliner to go into regular airline service

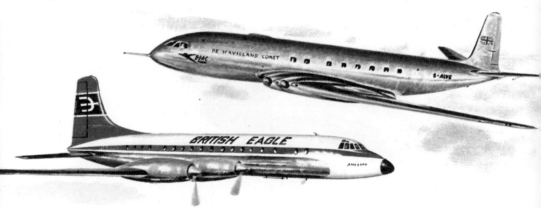

pure jet engines but they were cheaper to operate and the famous Vickers Viscounts and Bristol Britannias were powered by them.

But jet airline travel was not to be without its problems. In 1954 there was a series of accidents involving the Comet. These were the result, it was discovered, of metal fatigue,

Above: The Bristol Britannia turbo-prop airliner which still operates on some long-distance routes

Below: The American Boeing 707 was the first of the really big jet airliners

Above: A four-engined British
VC-10 with its engines mounted
at the rear of the aircraft,
beneath the tail

a phenomenon caused by the very high pressurisation needed in the Comet for flying at heights around 30,000 ft. Before the fault could be remedied both Russia and America introduced their own jet airliners, the twin-engined Russian Tu-104 and the American Boeing 707, which was the first, and so far the most successful, of the big four-engined jets.

Britain had lost her lead in the jet airliner race and one that she so far has not been able to regain. But in spite of the set-back the new

Above: The French Caravelle was the first of the jets to be built with its two engines at the rear of the aircraft

Comet 4 entered service and became the first jet airliner to operate on a trans-Atlantic route between London and New York.

As the fifties gave way to the sixties, new and quite revolutionary designs in jet passenger aircraft came along, like the French Caravelle which sported two Rolls-Royce engines set one at each side of the rear of the fuselage beneath the tail-plane. This had one enormous advantage over aircraft with wing-mounted engines, in that it allowed the wings to perform their basic function of 'lift' without being hindered by engines.

Below: The Douglas DC-8 was built as a rival for the Boeing 707 and is in service with Air Canada on its trans-Atlantic route

Above: The biggest passenger aircraft in the world is the Boeing 747 Jumbo jet which is capable of carrying up to 490 passengers

Then came the series of tri-jet airliners, like Britain's Trident and the Boeing 727, which had a cluster of three engines at the rear of the fuselage, with the top one operating through the tail itself.

Another variation of the rear-engined design came with Britain's VC-10, which has four engines in two pairs at either side of the rear of the fuselage.

Left: Of all the mighty jet aeroplanes, this one is the biggest – the Lockheed Galaxy, which can carry a payload of 118 tons up to almost 3,000 miles without refuelling

The coming of the 1970s brought the introduction of one of the biggest aircraft of all – the Jumbo. These flying behemoths, like the Lockheed Galaxy, which is the biggest aircraft in the world, can carry enormous payloads. The Boeing 747 passenger Jumbo can carry as many as 490 people on trans-Atlantic routes and has a cabin which is 20 ft. wide and 8 ft. high. It is the giant jets like the 747, with their great passenger capacity, which might help solve the problem of our cluttered skies.

Below: This aircraft, steadily increasing in popularity with airlines throughout the world, is the three-engined Boeing 727

Left: The world's first super-sonic transport aircraft to fly was the Russian Tu-144 which took to the air in 1960. It is designed to travel at more than twice the speed of sound and carry up to 121 passengers

Supersonic Airliners

Half a century ago no-one could have imagined even in their wildest dreams that one day aircraft would be built which could carry people at twice the speed of sound, and yet, within a few years from now, the Anglo-French Concorde will be doing just that.

It was the Russians who first succeeded in flying a supersonic airliner and that was as long ago as 1960. Their supersonic aircraft is the Tu-144, which is designed to carry up to 121 passengers at speeds up to 1,550 m.p.h.

The Anglo-French Concorde which first flew in 1969 is bigger and capable of carrying a few more passengers but is slightly slower with a maximum speed of around 1,450 m.p.h.

Below: A look into the future of passenger travel in space. The illustration shows the Martin Space transporter, which would be used rather like a rocket to shoot other craft into space. It would use rockets for take-off and turbo-fans for the return journey to Earth. Although this is still on the drawing board, one day it might take passengers into space

Man is on the brink of regular supersonic travel and it is fair to suppose that it will not stop there. Airliners will undoubtedly reach great speeds, possibly even as much as 5000 m.p.h., which would cut down trans-Atlantic travelling time to under 45 minutes – less time than it now takes to fly from London to Edinburgh!

Manned flights to the moon are regarded as almost commonplace now and the possibility of sending passenger-carrying craft into space is no longer as ridiculous and impracticable as it once seemed.

After all, it is not so long ago that man was unable to fly at all. The young people who today live in this exciting age of space exploration might well become the space travellers of tomorrow.

Above: The Anglo-French Concorde is the Western World's contribution to supersonic passenger travel. Although not as fast as its Russian counterpart, it is built to carry more passengers and is expected to come into service within the next few years. Concorde is seen here landing with its special droop nose down to give the captain clear vision

INDEX Page numbers in italics refer to illustrations and captions